pocket posh®
· · · · · · · · · ·
take care

Inspired Activities
for **Calm**

Andrews McMeel
PUBLISHING®

We all need some time to focus on ourselves. It's easy to become overwhelmed—by work, by home responsibilities, by the news of the day. It's important to step away, relax, and recenter. *Take Care: Inspired Activities for Calm* invites you to practice small moments of self-care through mindful activities, inspirational words, and thought-provoking journal prompts. Take some time for yourself.

. . . take care.

"Sometimes the most important thing in a whole day is the rest we take between two deep breaths."

—*Etty Hillesum*

```
L E A R L G R E Y T E A G L J C T E U T
V O L A S W I J O F R L T U K B A N U E
D H O T F T F K L I Z T E J A L O G B A
I U C S O O L O N G T E A L L K D L L P
Y L X E E I L S S Q G M B E F U A I A O
A D N B M L J M S U F K A M L T R S C T
K T L I G R E E N T E A G O A A J H K Q
W H I T E T E A T G J O S N V R E B T W
D U T M I K B G F M J T A L O O E R E W
M T E A B A L L I N F U S E R M L E A P
U F I R F Y R H S X A F R X Y A I A H C
S M V S Z A G S T R A I N E R T N K T A
L F K I G H Z Y O Y J V T D S I G F H F
I I E U O F N B P A F Y E A T C T A O F
N N S F I L T E R E D W A T E R E S A E
B I H O N E Y L T F N N C T E X A T W I
A S I Q K H G B A Y G J U Z P X M T L N
G H O V C E E C J D E J P L I Y P E L E
S G J I M R E Z A D M D L Z N C M A A P
C O M P L E X R C D M C K Y G T L Q J J
```

the art of tea

AROMATIC

BLACK TEA

CAFFEINE

COMPLEX

DARJEELING TEA

EARL GREY TEA

ENGLISH BREAKFAST
TEA

FILTERED WATER

FINISH

FLAVOR

GREEN TEA

HONEY

LEMON

LOOSE LEAF

MILK

MUSLIN BAGS

OOLONG TEA

STEEPING

STRAINER

SUGAR

TEA BAGS

TEA BALL INFUSER

TEACUP

TEAPOT

WHITE TEA

golden thread breathing

Breath is our life force; it centers us, it grounds us. Golden Thread Breathing is an ancient technique that aids relaxation. When you breathe more deeply, it calms your entire body and it helps clear your mind.

STEP 1: Find a comfortable position in a supportive chair, sit cross-legged on a cushion, or even lie down . . . whatever's most relaxing for you.

. . . .

STEP 2: Breathe in through your nose, and then out through your relaxed, slightly open mouth. Try breathing out for longer than you breathe in.

. . . .

STEP 3: As you breathe out, imagine a thin golden thread unfurling with your breath. Visualize it unfurling farther and farther, for as long as you are exhaling. Focus on this image.

. . . .

STEP 4: Try to extend your thread on your exhalations. Repeat the visualization and breathing for two to five minutes.

. . . .

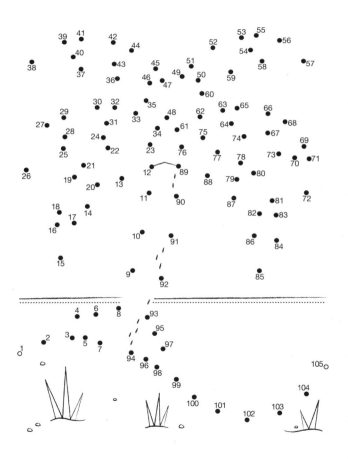

practicing gratitude

Practicing gratitude has been proven to improve emotional and physical health. When we take the time to stop and appreciate the good in our lives, we reframe our perspective. Expressing gratitude, even for the smallest things, can lead to big change.

What is something in your physical environment that you are grateful for, for example your favorite piece of art, a treasured family heirloom, even a comfy chair?

. . . .

. . . .

. . . .

. . . .

. . . .

. . . .

. . . .

"Nourishing yourself in a way that helps you blossom in the direction you want to go is attainable, and you are worth the effort."

—Deborah Day

Forest Bathing By Fred Piscop

ACROSS

1. __ for (choose)
4. Bro's sibling
7. A forest bathing activity: __-spring therapy
10. While forest bathing, breathe in the fresh, clean __
11. Unrefined metal
12. Italy's continent: Abbr.
13. Herbal beverage
14. Fleming who created 007
15. Enjoyed dinner
16. Not moving at all
18. __ Hawkins Day
20. Pie __ mode
21. All stressed out
22. "__ you!" (response to a sneeze)
24. Made dove sounds
26. Period of history
29. Quotable Yankee Yogi
30. Colorful blooms, for short
32. Fruity beverage
33. Kilmer who played Batman
35. Mauna __, Hawaii
36. "The way of nature"
37. Poet's "before"
38. "Nature" network
39. Fractions of days: Abbr.
40. Sault __ Marie, Mich.
41. "For __ a jolly good ..."

DOWN

1. Morsels in granola
2. Michelangelo statue at St. Peter's
3. Nature __ (place to hike)
4. A sensory pleasure while forest bathing is the smell of damp __
5. Nest egg investment: Abbr.
6. Forest bathing stimulates the __
7. Coin-flip option
8. Protruding navel
9. While forest bathing, you may enjoy the scent of a __
17. Part of a repair bill
19. Adams who photographed nature
21. Williams in Cooperstown
23. When forest bathing, you may enjoy the sunlight shining through the __
24. Aromatic 9-Down that you may enjoy while forest bathing
25. Twistable Nabisco cookies
27. "Nature" essayist __ Waldo Emerson
28. Sun-baked brick
29. In Japanese, shinrin-yoku means "forest __"
30. Great delight

31. Talk fresh to
34. "All nature is but __":
    Alexander Pope

"Instead of thinking outside the box, get rid of the box."

—Deepak Chopra

```
P O R T S M O U T H W N Z Z X H K S F H
K W C L A C O N N E R G U S E P Q Z N Y
C P I N E I S L A N D R E J E T S J E F
A B A C V R Q C Y V C W E J L X F X D Y
W K O Y A T V E C A E I S F K A R N A L
E P P O J Y L B T L H J A R T C A B U A
H V E O T G U N G C D C B I D L N B T H
N C H A N H A C A M E M N S S O A R I A
L V W A M S B E O P Q A X I O M S I O I
V R L F O A B A O S Z T H M Z I T G I N
O N X W I N N T Y N W A F E K C O H S A
H H P O O F I Q A H W L C V A O R T L C
K N W N S L P M D A A I E Y Q R I O E H
X E N I A J P W I H N R U D Z O A N O A
W A L S W I C K I E B A B V G L R E F T
C O U X H T I M V X C O R O Y L J I H H
B A M A R B L E H E A D R O R A A O O A
S B A R H A R B O R V S E D V B S K P M
A Y R O C K P O R T B P P R N V M V E T
H F Z T B I G S U R P Y Q L V I Y L Z Z
```

coastal towns

ASTORIA	HALF MOON BAY	OIA
BAR HARBOR	ISLE OF HOPE	PINE ISLAND
BIG SUR	KIAWAH ISLAND	PORTSMOUTH
BOOTHBAY HARBOR	LA CONNER	ROCKPORT
BRIGHTON	LAHAINA	SANTA CRUZ
CANNON BEACH	LANGLEY	SAUSALITO
CAYUCOS	LEWES	VENICE
CHATHAM	MANZANITA	
COROLLA	MARBLEHEAD	

```
T  B  G  U  I  T  A  R  Z  P  X  V
V  U  A  P  E  A  C  H  R  O  T  I
D  B  B  N  Z  X  O  A  N  M  E  O
R  U  Z  A  J  L  H  A  P  A  P  L
U  L  X  K  L  O  I  Z  I  N  M  I
M  L  C  E  H  P  X  J  Z  G  U  N
P  I  C  C  O  L  O  Y  Z  O  R  C
Y  B  N  E  C  T  A  R  A  Y  T  H
```

find and circle

Ten musical instruments	⊘○○○○○○○○○
Two five-letter fruits	○○
It's collected by bees	○
Restaurant chain: ____ Hut	○
Rodeo animal	○

"Change your thoughts,

and you change your world."

—*Norman Vincent Peale*

clear sky meditation

Imagine inner peace, calm, and quietude as a clear blue sky. Visualize the sky. Like clouds, intrusive thoughts—to-do lists, anxieties, negative self-talk—may come, but the sky itself, our potential for mindfulness and clarity, remains constant. Let the clouds blow through. Concentrate on the sky.

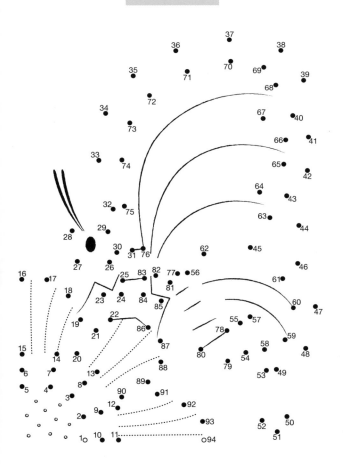

practicing gratitude

We are all so busy that it's easy to accumulate stress, but taking time to decompress is essential to our mental and physical well-being. What are five things that relax you? Write them below. Can you make the time to do one of these things today?

1. . . . .

2. . . . .

3. . . . .

4. . . . .

5. . . . .

"Invent your world.
Surround yourself
with people, color,
sounds, and work
that nourish you."

—*Susan Ariel Rainbow Kennedy*

MEDITATION By Fred Piscop

ACROSS

1. With 6-Across, what meditation seeks to achieve
6. See 1-Across
11. Dudley of "Arthur"
12. Respected villager
13. Nile River dam
14. Fudd of cartoons
15. Intent look
17. Muscular fitness
20. Hindu or Buddhist script dealing with meditation
24. One skilled in CPR
25. Extra bed in a hotel room
26. Give assistance to
27. Place for a guru to meditate
29. Cries out loud
30. Initial stage
32. Hindu god often depicted meditating
35. Some lo-cal brews
39. Urge forward
40. Totally pointless
41. Mannerless sorts
42. Curly-tailed Japanese dog

5. Monopoly payment
6. Eye intently
7. DeGeneres of TV talk
8. Naval honcho: Abbr.
9. So-so grade
10. Make a blunder
16. Molecule components
17. Drink with crumpets
18. Meditative chants
19. To the __ degree (extremely)
21. Meditative Chinese philosophy
22. Barbecue morsel
23. Annoying online pop-ups
25. Suez and Panama, for two
28. Nomadic sort
29. Smell something fierce
31. Charles Lamb's alias
32. Bro or sis
33. Managed care plan: Abbr.
34. Wall St. debut
36. __ chi (meditative martial art)
37. Dr. who treats sinus issues
38. Baltic or Caspian

DOWN

1. The Monkees' "__ Believer"
2. Sudoku box fillers: Abbr.
3. The __ (what meditators try to live in)
4. Wipe clean

"Choose, everyday, to forgive
yourself. You are human,
flawed, and most of all
worthy of love."

—Alison Malee

```
L D N V H U M O R L N Q K L B X P F M S
R A E Q V S L M S O B O U N T Y L V Q T
S A F L V T D R I I Q K V D I Y E T L T
H E G S I Q J T E Y E A F B E V A V C K
N E A P X G A G T M E K S H M R S V A I
T S N Y X N H I J V U W V I M V U K T R
X P A J I P S T I G F N H V R J R M E P
R Z A L O O P S Z U R W E A N O E T R A
F E C O R Y S P T N J A H R L N E Y Q M
W N W E K E Z B S R B L T C A G J N R P
I T N A C L W Y I E L D B I O T S H H E
W E O X R A F I Q S Y H U I F D E Z Z R
G R E B X D F H F T O Q K Y B Y D R Z W
D T V S I X T G A R H C B Z S A E L Z X
D A G S A T I S F A C T I O N E B Z E Z
F I I N A F B D X I P W U B G K W Y D C
Y N Q H T R E A T N L U K E U W C S Z O
R J X O F R E E R E I N U L I O Q Y S X
I S D E S I R E R D S A T I S F Y D E E
N N L E N I E N C Y E G O V O H Y D T L
```

indulge

BABY
BOUNTY
CATER
CODDLE
DELIGHT
DESIRE
ENJOY
ENTERTAIN
EXCESSIVE

FREE REIN
GENEROSITY
GRATIFY
HUMOR
INCLINATION
LENIENCY
PAMPER
PLEASURE
REMUNERATE

REWARD
SATISFACTION
SATISFY
TREAT
UNRESTRAINED
WHIM
YIELD

create space

Saying no can be hard, but in order to reach our fullest potential we must leave space in our lives for rest, for resetting our mindset, for new ideas and experiences. What can you say no to that might create that space?

. . . .

. . . .

. . . .

. . . .

. . . .

. . . .

. . . .

. . . .

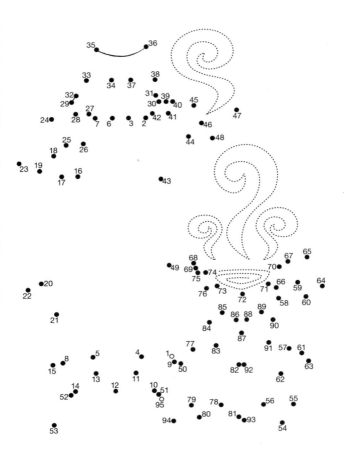

31

mindful breathing

STEP 1: Sit in a comfortable chair or on a cushion. Close your eyes. Pay attention to your breathing.

. . . .

STEP 2: Place your hand on your stomach. Think about how it expands and contracts as you breathe. Tune into the sensation.

. . . .

STEP 3: Take a long, deep breath in through your nose, trying to fill your lungs completely. Hold for two seconds and then breathe everything out through your mouth.

. . . .

STEP 4: Try to send your breath where you feel any tension or pain. Breathe in softness, looseness. Breathe out tightness, discomfort.

. . . .

STEP 5: Feel your muscles relax as you continue to breathe in relaxation and breathe out tension.

. . . .

STEP 6: When you are ready, take a slow, deep breath in and begin to "wake up" different parts of your body. Start by wiggling your fingers and toes, and work your way toward your heart.

. . . .

"Love is the great miracle
cure. Loving ourselves works
miracles in our lives."

—*Louise L. Hay*

NEW AGE By Fred Piscop

ACROSS

1. One-named Irish New Ager
5. New Age pianist John
9. Has to have
11. Popular New Age instrument
12. Playful aquatic mammal
13. Second U.S. president John
14. Penne or rigatoni
16. "Hey, you!"
19. New Age healer
23. Chimp or gorilla
24. Face card's value in blackjack
25. Eggs on sushi rolls
26. New Age music often incorporates the sounds of __
28. New Age band the __ Winter Consort
29. Taken-back autos, for short
31. New Age music is sometimes scorned as "yuppie __"
34. Ankle-length skirts
38. Some German autos
39. Pizza serving
40. Bowler's target
41. "Tubular Bells," by __ Oldfield, was an early New Age album

DOWN

1. Brian who has produced many New Age albums
2. Tennis court divider
3. "Are we there __?"
4. Highly skilled
5. __ wave (destructive water)
6. Approximate landing time: Abbr.
7. America's "uncle"
8. Fractions of days: Abbr.
10. Mrs., in Mexico
11. "... __ a tuffet"
15. Bo Peep's flock
16. Two-thumbs-down review
17. Relaxing place where New Age music may be heard
18. "Game, __, match"
20. New Age pianist __ Stein
21. Almost-worthless French coin
22. No. on a business card
24. Long, hard journeys
27. Range separating Europe from Asia
28. Sacred song of David
30. Chants from New Agers
31. Deck-swabber's implement
32. News org. since 1958

33. Tony Scott's "Music for ___ Meditation" is considered to be the first New Age recording
35. Numeral at the top of a sundial
36. "That's disgusting!"
37. Get a glimpse of

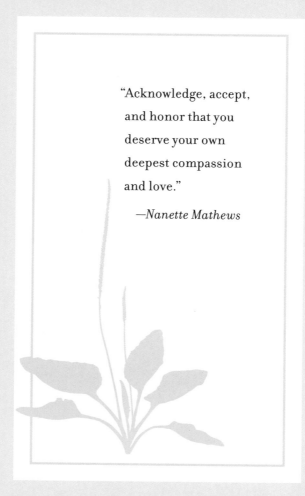

"Acknowledge, accept, and honor that you deserve your own deepest compassion and love."

—*Nanette Mathews*

```
O F P E O N Y K P Z J C H I B I S C U S
E R E A K C A R N A T I O N W I A S S C
B E Y G H Y P N R U I Q D R V B I N B W
V E K I R Y R H I I X L N J I M N A I A
A S V H R E M Q L A Z I H F P Q E P F Y
R I Z C Y I C I G O E I G A A J D D B W
S A N K E D S A R R X P T N D K R R R O
A K Z O L P R V L D E I T B P J A A E N
P I B E G A J A K S E W G E W U G G W U
C J N E P E R B N N E L O D E Z R O O G
A R C N D S B K S G A N P L Z W V N L E
L E P J I V P M S D E N N K F G S G F S
L D D P B Z A V I P Q A W A E N C O L U
A N A M W R P O U I U K S R N U U H L S
L E F Z I X L B Z L L R B O I E U S E S
I V F G F U T K S U Q E N A S T E R B I
L A O C S K N L Y T R C A L I L M U L C
Y L D B F U V X W A O E U G C Y M J Q R
D G I G V I H T A E R B S Y B A B F F A
I N L H K T O N E M T E G R O F J Y I N
```

flowers

ASTER	GARDENIA	MARIGOLD
BABY'S BREATH	GERBERA	NARCISSUS
BEGONIA	GLADIOLUS	PEONY
BELLFLOWER	HIBISCUS	PHLOX
CALLA LILY	HYDRANGEA	QUEEN ANNE'S LACE
CARNATION	IMPATIENS	SNAPDRAGON
DAFFODIL	IRIS	SUNFLOWER
DAHLIA	LARKSPUR	SWEET PEA
FORGET-ME-NOT	LAVENDER	TULIP
FREESIA	LILAC	ZINNIA

```
L Z O R A N G E K J W I
V Y N O O N L G S O A N
I L N Z J K N E A H Y D
O I Z X V I I M M N N I
L B C H M R A L Z U E G
E R X M A L J X I V R O
T A E K L M A R O O N Y
K L P U R P L E H Z N C
```

find and circle

Five mammals starting with "L"	⊘ ○ ○ ○ ○
Five six-letter colors	○ ○ ○ ○ ○
Two five-letter Zodiac signs	○ ○
Marion Morrison's stage name: ____ ____	○ ○
Midday time	○

"Caring for your body, mind, and spirit is your greatest and grandest responsibility. It's about listening to the needs of your soul and then honoring them."

—*Kristi Ling*

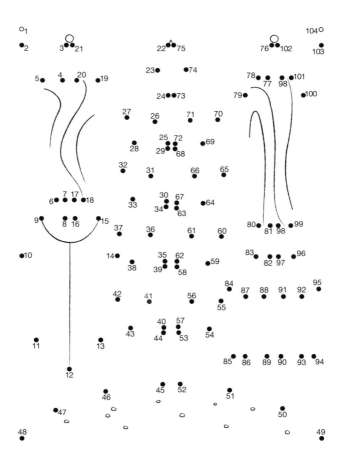

"To accept ourselves as we are
means to value our imperfections
as much as our perfections."

—*Sandra Bierig*

Reading By Fred Piscop

ACROSS

1. Enjoy a buffet
4. Hoops org.
7. Place for a massage
10. Fruity beverage suffix
11. Sculler's need
12. Treater's pickup
13. 9-Down, to Eve
14. Smelter input
15. Copy mindlessly
16. Something for a Kindle owner to read
18. Reading a novel offers a relaxing __ from the real world
20. Make a blunder
21. One with a piggy bank
22. Biscotti flavoring
24. Reading __ tales can be relaxing for parents and children
26. Greek P
29. Spring up
30. Dance lesson components
32. No longer edible
33. 1953-61 presidential monogram
35. Have a bug
36. Tell a whopper
37. Place to graze
38. Messenger __ (genetic material)
39. Pull the plug on
40. Dr. concerned with otitis or rhinitis
41. President pro __

DOWN

1. Reading is a good way to __ tension
2. Sun-dried brick
3. Sax bigger than an alto
4. A reading __ in your home is a good place to relax
5. Some people relax here with a book and a beer
6. Places to play or fight
7. Barrel slat
8. Coffee, a bagel and the Sunday __ make for a relaxing routine
9. Brother of Cain
17. Paperless exams
19. Out in the open
21. Sib's nickname
23. Phonograph arm attachment
24. Reading on a __ can be relaxing pre-work activity
25. Lent a hand to
27. Reading is known to reduce one's __ rate
28. Voice a point of view
29. Up the the task

30. A window __ in one's home
    is a great place to read
31. Enjoy a relaxing night out
    by reading at a poetry __
34. Relaxing room to read in

"Love yourself enough to set boundaries. Your time and energy are precious. You get to choose how you use it. You teach people how to treat you by deciding what you will and won't accept."

—*Anna Taylor*

```
F R E N C H S I L K P I E R G M C F F B
C H E R R Y S T R U D E L T I U H N C A
S T E A C A K E I M I Q C B S Q E C Q K
T F F L G T S T A G S Y D P I C E J R E
I W J N E V A C U C Z J U H W R S U K D
C A R A S P B E R R Y S C O N E E S N G
K D E T Z Z H S W E N Z D C P A D U Q O
Y G M J D H N A H T N O N H H M A G M O
B Y M P B I L L N O A L V O M P N A A D
U I T T F C E F O T M D T E H U I R D S
N P P F R B R R A C E E T G R F S C E C
K W U A B I A F W P A A M A K F H O D R
R M E Q A C W G R I K N R A R G E O A O
I B Y L A O H Z E F L A N C D T H K I I
N L C M B R U G E L A C H O O E L I L S
G E D O U G H N U T S L S A L O G E Y S
L C I N N A M O N R O L L N X I K S T A
E R B V P A P P L E F R I T T E R I S N
A R T I S A N B R E A D O Z G N C B E T
P E A C H G A L E T T E C U P C A K E S
```

bakery

APPLE FRITTER
ARTISAN BREAD
BAGELS
BAKED GOODS
BEAR CLAW
CANNOLI
CHEESE DANISH
CHERRY STRUDEL
CINNAMON ROLL
CREAM PUFF

CROISSANT
CUPCAKES
DOUGHNUTS
ÉCLAIR
ELEPHANT EAR COOKIE
FLAN
FRENCH SILK PIE
HOMEMADE
KRINGLE
MACAROON

MADE DAILY
MUFFINS
PEACH GALETTE
RASPBERRY SCONE
RUGELACH
STICKY BUN
SUGAR COOKIES
TARTLET
TEA CAKE
TURNOVER

4-7-8 breathing

This breathing exercise promotes relaxation.

STEP 1: Breathe in gently through your nose for four seconds.

. . . .

STEP 2: Hold for seven seconds.

. . . .

STEP 3: Breathe out through your mouth for eight seconds.

. . . .

STEP 4: Repeat this breath pattern until you feel calm.

. . . .

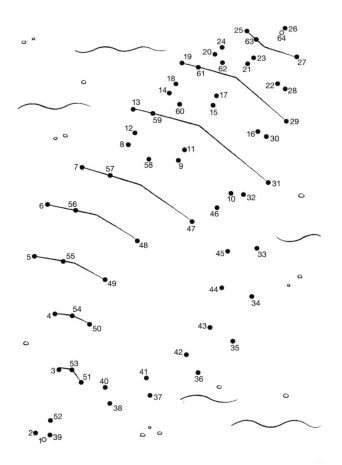

```
C  L  I  Q  U  I  D  Z  P  I  K  E
X  A  Z  P  M  A  R  L  I  N  V  S
T  P  R  K  E  T  X  T  H  B  D  A
U  A  Y  P  K  R  K  N  C  A  I  L
N  T  Z  R  Z  O  C  I  T  T  L  M
A  C  A  V  X  U  Y  H  I  C  O  O
Z  H  M  U  S  T  A  R  D  H  S  N
S  G  R  O  U  P  E  R  J  G  A  S
```

find and circle

Nine fish	⦿○○○○○○○○
Three forms of matter	○○○
Three five-letter words ending in "TCH"	○○○
Seven-letter hot dog topping	○
Clue or sign	○

"Do something nice for yourself today. Find some quiet, sit in stillness, breathe. Put your problems on pause. You deserve a break."

—*Akiroq Brost*

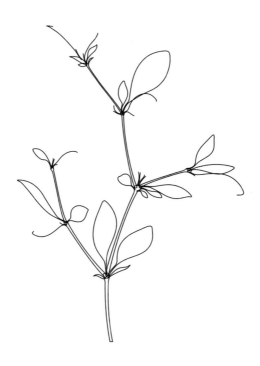

RELAX By Fred Piscop

ACROSS

1. Taking __, deep breaths can relax you
5. Do a mental body __ as a way to relax
9. Airline with "flying boats," once
11. For a relaxing outdoor experience, forest __
12. Assists in wrongdoing
13. Sensational, like tabloid headlines
14. Provoke with a dare
16. Practice in a boxing ring
19. Honors with playful insults
23. Bylaw, for short
24. Relax in the afternoon with a short __
25. __ de toilette (perfume)
26. Trample underfoot
28. __ out a window to relax
29. Marriage site
31. Like a superbly pitched ballgame
34. Find a blind date for
38. Relax by allowing yourself some __ time
39. Increase your __ rate with exercise, it'll have a relaxing effect
40. Understands, as a joke
41. One of Columbus's ships

DOWN

1. Place to relax and be pampered
2. Chem or bio room
3. __-hit wonder
4. Splashing cold __ on your face can relax you
5. Relax in this hot, steamy locale
6. Middle point: Abbr.
7. Tuna in sushi rolls
8. Homer Simpson's neighbor __ Flanders
10. Additive that lends a savory flavor to food
11. Softly hit fly ball
15. Union general Ulysses S. __
16. 4th-yr. students
17. Relax by cuddling with a __
18. Listening to New __ music can be relaxing
20. Mediterranean or Baltic
21. Whirling toon devil, familiarly
22. Seek damages from
24. Nick of "Cape Fear"
27. Aches and __
28. A cup of herbal __ tea can have a relaxing effect
30. Campfire residue
31. Has-been horse
32. Bullring cheer

33. Soaking in a __ tub will relax you
35. __ chi, a relaxing meditative exercise
36. Caterer's coffee vessel
37. School-supporting org.

"What we know matters, but who we are matters more."

—*Brené Brown*

```
J  W  S  G  R  A  Y  F  U  Z  Z  L
Z  A  I  H  S  Z  U  G  O  L  D  I
F  N  Z  N  R  U  N  T  X  J  Z  T
R  E  J  Z  T  I  M  B  U  V  M  H
I  E  K  Y  R  E  M  M  U  M  C  I
Z  R  V  P  C  J  R  P  E  Z  N  U
Z  G  S  I  L  I  C  O  N  R  Z  M
F  I  Z  Z  C  A  L  C  I  U  M  G
```

find and circle

Five words ending in "ZZ"	⊙○○○○
Four seasons	○○○○
Three seven-letter elements	○○○
Three colors starting with "G"	○○○
Six-letter crustacean	○

"The greatest thing about dreams is they don't expire. They can lay dormant for years and when you pull them out and dust them off, they shine like new."

—*Casi McLean*

```
A S V B U P K R E D N E V A L Z N R E T
F K C E L T Y N F O M K O M S F Y E U L
Q K W V G O Z O I U D G A W L K B B L A
E U A I P M O B M P C H E A A Q G M B Q
X J G L W R E Z D B O H R H W S B A Y F
O K C O C I L Q L G X O S Z V T W Y B Z
O R A N G E B A A T C D T I M K M M A B
C E N E T B C N F C K I U B A H Z T B V
H J E G N K Y E A E U L B Y K S O F T A
A Q E G E E C M T W I K V V Q C Y H S A
R K R P M A E D N O Z H W P I Y K P Y Q
T V G L E L Z R Z O A M Y R S I S I H U
R I T A R Y A R G J D N P W U C S Y T A
E P S N A E D X X Y S A I B T K D Q E M
U D E T L F S X D H L U L U E N S S M A
S U R E D V I O L E T L I E U U C A A R
E G O Y L S E F Y S U O E G C F R Q W I
Y W F P M T L Y P Z N S R K Q O T O N N
T G W Q D Z E F S Y Y U K F O N I T J E
X R D O V Z J E X N B W F N H X G P Y M
```

colors

AMBER
AMETHYST
APRICOT
AQUAMARINE
BABY BLUE
BEIGE
BLACK
BURGUNDY
CAMEL

CELADON
CHARTREUSE
CORAL
EGGPLANT
EMERALD
FOREST GREEN
FUCHSIA
GRAY
KELLY GREEN

LAVENDER
MAHOGANY
MAROON
OLIVE
ONYX
ORANGE
PINK
RED-VIOLET
SKY BLUE

R U C H A N D L E R V K
R O R B A P R I L X M T
A E S U L K N A C K O J
C T Z S G A J K K E N O
H I K J V U C C I G I E
E H K I N K A K C I C Y
L W M A R C H Y K E A C
Z P H O E B E J Z B L H

find and circle

Six *Friends* characters	⊘○○○○○
Three five-letter colors	○○○
Three words starting and ending in "K"	○○○
Two five-letter months	○○
Country with three "U"s	○

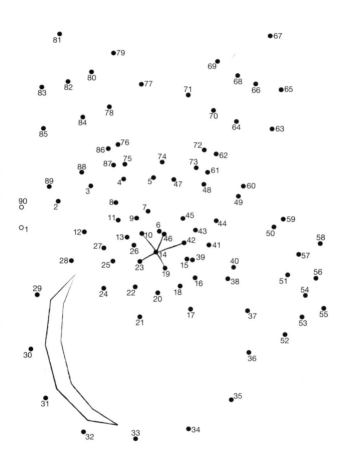

forest bathing

Forest bathing, or *shinrin-yoku*, is a Japanese term for mindfully spending time in nature. This screen-free wellness practice has gained newfound interest in our tech-obsessed times with good reason. Time spent away from modern distractions, appreciating whatever nature is available to you—whether on a structured meditative hike or a quick stroll around your own block—has undeniable benefits.

"Personality begins where comparison leaves off. Be unique. Be memorable. Be confident. Be proud."

—*Shannon L. Alder*

find and circle

Eight mammals ending in "E"	⊘○○○○○○○
Four four-letter units of length	○○○○
Star Wars creator (first/last name)	○○
Increase your bet in poker	○
Aviator	○

"Learning to love yourself is like learning to walk—essential, life-changing, and the only way to stand tall."

—*Vironika Tugaleva*

sensory By Fred Piscop

ACROSS

1. The scent of __ oil relaxes the body and is a sleep aid
5. Pirate's plunder
9. You can command __ to play relaxing sounds on your Echo device
11. Sounds of the __, such as waves and seagulls, can relax you
12. "Do you __?" (query after a joke)
13. In deplorable condition
14. The scent of this fruit can reduce stress and anxiety
16. Candles scented with this herb can have a relaxing effect
19. Convert into charged particles
23. Long __ (in the past)
24. Antlered beast
25. Lavender __, applied during a massage, has a relaxing aroma
26. Harrison of the Beatles
28. Has a late meal
29. Aromatherapy for medicinal use was practiced in this ancient land
31. Wolfgang Puck's flagship eatery

34. The aroma of jasmine can lower your __ rate and help you sleep
38. __ chamomile is a well-known calming agent
39. Presentations at expos, for short
40. Distance between bridge supports
41. Candles scented with this tree can have a relaxing effect

DOWN

1. Cleaning cloth
2. Bullring cheer
3. "Game, __, match"
4. Banish from one's homeland
5. Country singer Rimes
6. Granola morsel
7. Halloween mo.
8. "Love __ neighbor"
10. Enjoyed a smorgasbord
11. The sound of a babbling __ is calming
15. "Wrecking Ball" singer Cyrus
16. Lose firmness, as a mattress
17. Listening to New __ music has a calming effect
18. Icky stuff
20. Debtor's note

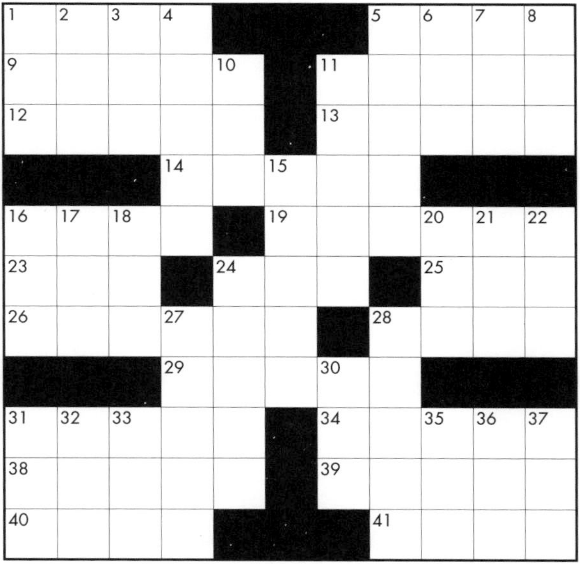

21. __ code (address part)
22. Overhead rails
24. Incite into pulling a prank, say
27. A daughter of King Lear
28. Nearly vertical, as a cliff
30. Deg. for many a professor
31. 4th-yr. students
32. The __ of burning wood is a relaxing sound
33. Org. for M.D.s
35. "__ seeing things"
36. Harry Potter pal Weasley
37. Monogram of the inspiration for "Cats"

"The challenge is
not to be perfect . . .
it's to be whole."

—*Jane Fonda*

```
L H C V C K C Z L A J R
P I A H B H C O I Y E X
T U O I I Z E D U H N A
I C M N T L N E T G N X
G O X A V I E N T I A Z
E K J A G U A R H A Z R
R E N T S P I C E S H X
L E O P A R D P E P S I
```

find and circle

Nine felines	⦸○○○○○○○○
Four five-letter countries	○○○○
Two competing cola brands	○○
Thyme, oregano, and cinnamon, for example	○
Lease	○

practice good (sleep) hygiene

Having a bedtime routine is not just for babies. Good sleep hygiene makes for a better-rested, happier daytime for everyone. Here are some tips for a calmer bedtime:

Try to keep a schedule. Going to bed and waking up around the same time every day helps your body acclimate to your specific rhythms. With your body on board, you'll fall asleep easier.

. . . .

Go screen-free in bed. Glowing screens are not relaxing.

. . . .

Create an end-of-day routine. Starting thirty minutes before bed, begin to wind down, maybe with a good book, maybe with a short meditation. Make a mindful shift toward sleep.

. . . .

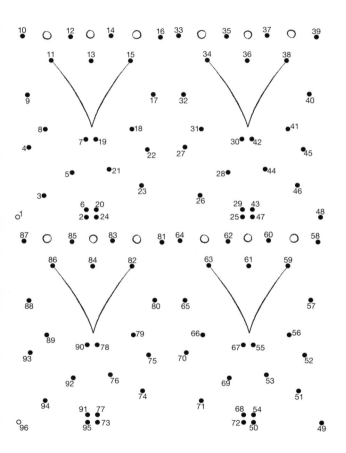

83

"Instructions for living a life:

Pay attention.

Be astonished.

Tell about it."

—*Mary Oliver*

practicing gratitude

It is easy to lose our sense of awe about the world and our lives. But we are surrounded by miracles, big and small, every day—from a moment of connection with a friend to the vast expanse of the night sky. What astonishes you?

. . . .

. . . .

. . . .

. . . .

. . . .

. . . .

. . . .

. . . .

Spa By Fred Piscop

ACROSS

1. English spa city
5. __ scrub (spa treatment)
9. Spa at Lake Geneva, France
11. AM or FM
12. Big name in tractors
13. "The Age of Anxiety" poet W.H.
14. Mark who created Tom Sawyer
16. A spa is a place for some "me __"
19. Dinnerware dishes
23. Hawaiian stringed instrument, for short
24. Tax-collecting org.
25. A spa is a place to escape the __ race
26. Poet's "Get lost!"
28. Breezy and open
29. Twangy-voiced
31. An upscale one may have a spa
34. Shooting marble
38. Best possible
39. Sultan's women
40. Chemical __ (spa treatment)
41. Greek H's

DOWN

1. Tanning __ (spa amenity)
2. "__ Maria" (hymn)
3. Reason to play overtime
4. Bret who wrote "The Luck of Roaring Camp"
5. Spa amenity with hot rocks
6. Find a sum
7. Tell a whopper
8. Heavy weight
10. __ Age (music commonly played at a spa)
11. Train tracks
15. __-ski (time to enjoy a spa, perhaps)
16. Hot __ (spa amenity)
17. President Eisenhower, informally
18. "Little Women" woman
20. Prefix meaning "three"
21. __ candling (spa offering)
22. Pig's home
24. Counting everything
27. Hoops great Shaq
28. __ wrap (spa treatment)
30. Satisfied sound from a spa visitor
31. __-hop music
32. Poem of praise
33. Shirt with a slogan
35. Gallery contents
36. Drink with crumpets
37. Bad __ (German spa)

"No one is you, and that
is your superpower."

—*Elyse Santilli*

```
P C A M E R O O N E G G
Z E C K E T H I O P I A
J S R V C H I C K E N Y
L P D U R I C E Z J G A
A A U R A O A B O V E W
P I S H R I M P X K R R
E N V O D E N M A R K O
N K M E C U A D O R C N
```

find and circle

Nine countries	⊘○○○○○○○○
Fried ____	○○○○
____ ale (six-letter answer)	○
Opposite of below	○
Intangible quality; atmosphere	○

93

"Whatever anybody says or does, assume positive intent. You will be amazed at how your whole approach to a person or problem becomes very different."

—*Indra Nooyi*

find and circle

Six units of length	⊘○○○○○
Six five-letter words ending in "IGHT"	○○○○○○
Member of The Who (first/last name)	○○
Olivia ____-____ in *Grease*	○○
London landmark: Piccadilly ____	○

"We delight in the beauty of the butterfly, but rarely admit the changes it has gone through to achieve that beauty."

—*Maya Angelou*

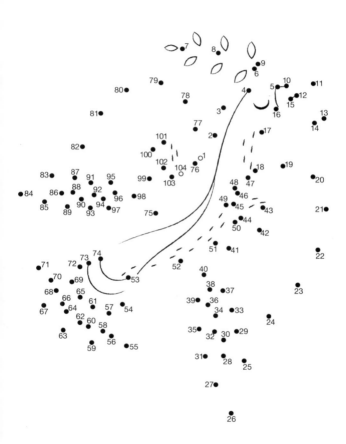

practicing gratitude

Our relationship with ourselves is the most meaningful one we can nurture, but we don't often treat ourselves as well as we should. Try to think about yourself the way you think about your loved ones. What are five positive qualities you have? Use encouraging, loving language.

1. . . . .

2. . . . .

3. . . . .

4. . . . .

5. . . . .

"To be happy—one must
find one's bliss."

—*Gloria Vanderbilt*

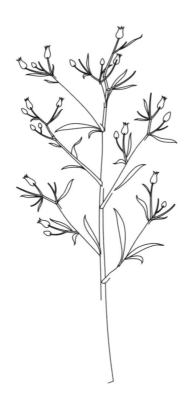

zen By Fred Piscop

ACROSS

1. The Beat __ were interested in Zen
6. Call a halt to
10. "Gone With the Wind" surname
11. Skylit lobbies
12. Zen is often practiced in the __ position
13. The __ Show's "Moment of Zen"
14. Tee, polo or tank top
16. Zen is a __ of Buddhism
19. Pine leaf
23. Golden-years investment: Abbr.
24. Beaver's construction
25. Nothing at all
26. Enlightenment, in Zen
28. What "zen," as an adjective, means
29. Change shape, in sci-fi
31. An Eastern land where Zen is practiced
34. River of Rome
38. Without company
39. Battery terminal
40. Calf-length skirt
41. Escorted, as to a penthouse

DOWN

1. Elected official, for short
2. Cry of surprise
3. Chow down
4. Have confidence in
5. Scout uniform accessory
6. Mushin is a Zen __ of mind
7. Prefix meaning "three"
8. OPEC resource
9. Pick up the tab
11. Pertinent, in law
15. "The bombs bursting __ ..."
16. Bro's sibling
17. Period of history
18. Garfield is one
20. Crime lab evidence
21. Diminutive, in rap names
22. Shade tree
24. Pilotless drone
27. Citizen of Muscat, e.g.
28. Land where Zen originated
30. After-school orgs.
31. Traffic snarl
32. Muhammad of the ring
33. Peas container
35. Ritual prostration, or __, is an important element in Zen
36. School's website suffix
37. Sales pro

"Courage doesn't always roar. Sometimes courage is the quiet voice at the end of the day saying, 'I will try again tomorrow.'"

—*Mary Anne Radmacher*

notes

notes

solutions

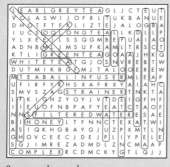

3   word search

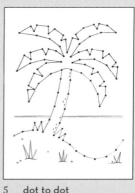

5   dot to dot

10   spot the differences

12   crossword

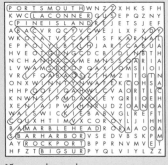

15 word search

TRUMPET, PICCOLO,
GUITAR, VIOLIN, PIANO,
BANJO, CELLO, TUBA,
DRUM, HARP—PEACH,
MANGO—NECTAR—
PIZZA—BULL

16 word roundup

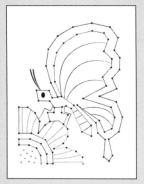

19 dot to dot

24 spot the differences

26 crossword

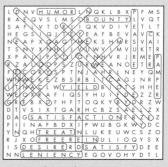

29 word search

31 dot to dot

36 spot the differences

38 crossword

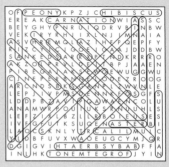

41 word search

LEMMING, LLAMA,
LEMUR, LION, LYNX—
VIOLET, ORANGE,
INDIGO, PURPLE,
MAROON—ARIES,
LIBRA—JOHN, WAYNE—
NOON

42 word roundup

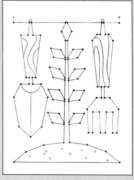

44 dot to dot

SOLUTIONS

48   spot the differences

E	A	T		N	B	A		S	P	A
A	D	E		O	A	R		T	A	B
S	O	N		O	R	E		A	P	E
E	B	O	O	K		N	O	V	E	L
	E	R	R		S	A	V	E	R	
		A	N	I	S	E				
	T	A	L	E	S		R	H	O	
A	R	I	S	E		S	T	E	P	S
B	A	D		D	D	E		A	I	L
L	I	E		L	E	A		R	N	A
E	N	D		E	N	T		T	E	M

50   crossword

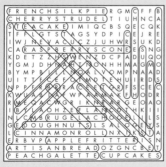

53   word search

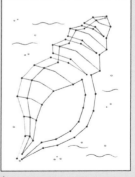

55   dot to dot

118

GROUPER, MARLIN,
SALMON, PERCH,
TROUT, SHARK, CARP,
TUNA, PIKE—LIQUID,
SOLID, GAS—BATCH,
PATCH, DITCH—
MUSTARD—HINT

57 word roundup

60 spot the differences

62 crossword

FRIZZ, JAZZ, BUZZ,
FUZZ, FIZZ—WINTER,
SPRING, SUMMER,
AUTUMN—CALCIUM,
SILICON, LITHIUM—
GREEN, GRAY, GOLD—
SHRIMP

65 word roundup

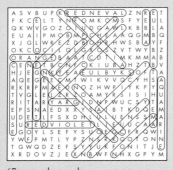

67 word search

CHANDLER, RACHEL,
MONICA, PHOEBE,
ROSS, JOEY—BLACK,
BEIGE, WHITE—KNACK,
KICK, KINK—MARCH,
APRIL—URUGUAY

68 word roundup

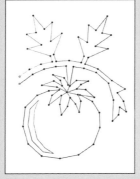

69 dot to dot

ANTELOPE, GIRAFFE,
GAZELLE, WHALE,
MOOSE, MOUSE, MULE,
APE—INCH, FOOT,
YARD, MILE—GEORGE,
LUCAS—RAISE—PILOT

74 word roundup

76 spot the differences

78 crossword

R	O	S	E				L	O	O	T
A	L	E	X	A		B	E	A	C	H
G	E	T	I	T		R	A	T	T	Y
			L	E	M	O	N			
S	A	G	E		I	O	N	I	Z	E
A	G	O		E	L	K		O	I	L
G	E	O	R	G	E		S	U	P	S
			E	G	Y	P	T			
S	P	A	G	O		H	E	A	R	T
R	O	M	A	N		D	E	M	O	S
S	P	A	N				P	I	N	E

LEOPARD, PANTHER,
CHEETAH, COUGAR,
JAGUAR, TIGER, LION,
LYNX, PUMA—CHINA,
CHILE, INDIA, HAITI—
PEPSI, COKE—SPICES—
RENT

81 word roundup

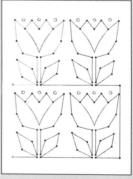

83 dot to dot

88 spot the differences

B	A	T	H				S	A	L	T
E	V	I	A	N		R	A	D	I	O
D	E	E	R	E		A	U	D	E	N
			T	W	A	I	N			
T	I	M	E		P	L	A	T	E	S
U	K	E		I	R	S		R	A	T
B	E	G	O	N	E		A	I	R	Y
			N	A	S	A	L			
H	O	T	E	L		A	G	A	T	E
I	D	E	A	L		H	A	R	E	M
P	E	E	L				E	T	A	S

90 crossword

CAMEROON, ETHIOPIA,
MOROCCO, ECUADOR,
DENMARK, NORWAY,
SPAIN, NEPAL, PERU—
CHICKEN, SHRIMP,
RICE, EGG—GINGER—
ABOVE—AURA

93 word roundup

FURLONG, METER, INCH,
MILE, YARD, FOOT—
NIGHT, FIGHT, MIGHT,
RIGHT, SIGHT, LIGHT—
PETE, TOWNSHEND—
NEWTON, JOHN—
CIRCUS

95 word roundup

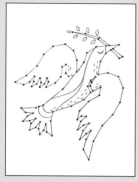

97 dot to dot

102 spot the differences

P	O	E	T	S			S	T	O	P
O	H	A	R	A		A	T	R	I	A
L	O	T	U	S		D	A	I	L	Y
		S	H	I	R	T				
S	E	C	T		N	E	E	D	L	E
I	R	A		D	A	M		N	I	L
S	A	T	O	R	I		C	A	L	M
		M	O	R	P	H				
J	A	P	A	N		T	I	B	E	R
A	L	O	N	E		A	N	O	D	E
M	I	D	I			S	A	W	U	P

104 crossword

108 spot the differences

Andrews McMeel Publishing
a division of Andrews McMeel Universal
1130 Walnut Street, Kansas City, Missouri 64106

www.andrewsmcmeel.com

20 21 22 23 24 RLP 10 9 8 7 6 5 4 3 2 1

ISBN: 978-1-5248-6053-0

Editor: Allison Adler
Art Director: Julie Barnes
Production Editor: Dave Shaw
Production Manager: Tamara Haus

ATTENTION: SCHOOLS AND BUSINESSES
Andrews McMeel books are available at quantity
discounts with bulk purchase for educational,
business, or sales promotional use. For information,
please e-mail the Andrews McMeel Publishing
Special Sales Department: specialsales@amuniversal.com.